Shots Across the Bow

Shots Across the Bow

A Two-Act Play

By Steve Herman

GRAVIER HOUSE PRESS
An Independent Publishing Company
New Orleans, Louisiana
2021

Library of Congress Publication Data:

Herman, Steve.
Shots Across the Bow / Steve Herman.
ISBN 978-1-7364501-2-3
Drama.

First Edition
2021

Published by:

Gravier House Press
P.O. Box 50337
New Orleans, LA 70150

Cover Design by: Becky Hicks, at Hoffman Miller

CAST

CONNIE, a woman, 50ish

BILL, Connie's husband, 50ish

JACOB, Connie's father, 75ish

TERRY, Jacob's friend, 75ish

JENNY, Connie's daughter, 20ish

CHARLES, Jenny's boyfriend, 25ish

BETTY, a woman, 50ish, Connie's friend

ACT ONE

Scene One.

Kitchen. Modest. Conventional. Bill is seated at a breakfast table, stirring a cup of coffee. Jenny is also seated at the table, eating cereal from a bowl. Connie is standing behind Bill, stage left, doing dishes at the sink.

CONNIE: When are you going to hear?

BILL: I don't know.

JENNY: Hear what?

CONNIE: I thought they were going to call you by 10:00?

JENNY: Hear what?

BILL: I don't know.

CONNIE: Weren't they meeting at 8:00?

BILL: I guess. Were supposed to.

JENNY: Hear what?

CONNIE: So why haven't they called?

BILL: I don't know.

    A brief silence.

JENNY: Hear what?

CONNIE: Nothing.

Connie comes around and sits at the breakfast table with Bill and Jenny. Bill lifts his cup of coffee. And then, to Jenny:

So when is Charles coming?

JENNY: I think he's supposed to be here around 1:00.

CONNIE: He is driving?

JENNY: Yep.

CONNIE: Are you nervous?

JENNY: No, I just feel like you guys hate him already.

BILL: How can I hate someone I haven't ever met?

JENNY: I hate tons of people I've never met.

> BILL, *lifting his coffee cup again, cracks a smile.*

CONNIE: We just want what's best for you.

JENNY: Don't you think so do I?

CONNIE: Well, I should tell you....

JENNY *stares 'what?' with her eyes.*

CONNIE: Um, your grandfather has invited Terry over again.

JENNY: Oh, Mom!

CONNIE: He's not so bad.

JENNY: It's so embarrassing.

CONNE: They're just old.

JENNY: And racist, and sexist, and homophobic, and-

CONNIE: Well, *(with a smile),* it'll be fun to see what your grandchildren think about you.

JENNY: Okay, hah hah, but why do they have to hang out here? Can't they hang out at Mr. Terry's?

BILL: Have you ever been to his place?

JENNY: Uh, not really.

BILL: Well.

JENNY: Well, what?

BILL: I mean the house itself is nice, -

CONNIE: He just isn't set up to have company, dear. Be charitable.

JENNY: I am. I just wish that you guys had been able to meet Chaz in some easier way.

CONNIE *says*: What do you mean, easier? *as* BILL *says*: Who's Chaz?

JENNY: Charles, dad. You know that. I call him 'Chaz'?

BILL: Good Christ.

JENNY: What?

BILL: Nothing.

CONNIE: What do you mean easier?

JENNY *(to Bill)*: What?!

BILL: Nothing.

CONNIE: We're having the kid over. What's so hard about that?

JENNY: You mean aside from Archie Bunker and his friend, Grady? *(CONNIE rolling eyes)* …. It's just too confined. We're trapped here. It's not like a reception or something where we can mingle or wander away. If things get uncomfortable, there's nowhere for him to go.

CONNIE *says*: Why would things get uncomfortable? *as* BILL *says:* Charles / Charlie / Chaz is free to jump on his scooter and turn around anytime he wants to leave.

JENNY *stands up in a huff and storms out of the kitchen.*

CONNIE: Great. Good job.

BILL: You don't like the idea of this kid any more than I do.

CONNIE: You're right; I don't. Don't care two shits about him. But if we're not careful, we are going to lose her. She'll run away with him. And we'll never get her back.

BILL: Don't be so pessimistic, dear. She'll be coming back after the divorce.

And he smiles. Connie half-smiles.

CONNIE: Funny. And but how old will our grandchildren be?

BILL *takes a deep breath.*

They each / both sip from their coffee cups.

CONNIE: So when do you think you will hear?

BILL: Don't know.

CONNIE: If you get it, we'll be moving anyway.

BILL *doesn't say anything.*

CONNIE: So maybe we'll lose her no matter what.

BILL: Nah.

CONNIE: But it's not the same.

BILL *(looks up at her, and, after a short pause)*: What do you mean?

long pause

CONNIE: Have you told her yet?

BILL: No. Have you?

CONNIE *shakes head 'No'. And then, after a pause*: You think they will be calling soon? To let us know?

BILL: I don't know.

CONNIE: They better give it to you. We might need that money to pay for a wedding.

BILL: Don't say that.

A silence.

CONNIE: I hope they call before this kid gets here. You think they will?

BILL *doesn't respond.*

CONNIE: Just don't understand what's taking so long(?)

BILL: I don't know.

Scene Two.

Living Room. Informal. (might, in some houses, where there is also a formal living room, be called a "TV Room" or the "Den") Charles is seated on the couch, center-stage, leaning forward, over his knees. Jacob is in a la-z-boy type recliner, stage left of the couch. There are two armchairs stage right of the couch, separated by a small end table. Bill is sitting on one of the chairs, Terry in the other. Presumably there is a television screen off-stage, where the audience is seated. Bill is half-listening to Charles. Jacob and Terry are focused on the would-be television screen.

CHARLES: So you see the Live 1975-1985 box set, and the record goes on the record player, *[with a deep announcer's voice, imitating:]* "Ladies and gentlemen, Bruce Springsteen and the E Street Band," and then Thunder Road, and the guy is working and slaving away, and but he gets on some website and he buys the tickets, and he takes a train plane automobile with his girlfriend to Broadway, because it's a once-in-a-lifetime chance.

BILL: The Bruce Springsteen show on Broadway?

CHARLES: Yeah, but when they get there, to the theatre, the tickets are counterfeit; and he can't believe it, and goes apeshit; and his girlfriend leaves him, dumps him; and he goes through all of these disheartening adventures, at first; but then he starts to have – reluctantly, begrudgingly – the best night of his life. And he meets some new cool hip chick who thinks Bruce Springsteen's a square, and she brings him to some cooler hipper little club that he thinks he is going to hate but begrudgingly starts to like. And maybe before that they go to some comedy show, and he begrudgingly hears something funny, and human, and perceptive; and then in the corner of this little club, at four in the morning, is Bruce Springsteen, just sitting there in the audience, and they call him up, and at first he refuses, or at least mock refuses, but then they keep pressing, and he finally begrudgingly, or at least pretend begrudgingly, is dragged up, and sings (not a Broadway song, but) Livin Proof.

BILL *takes it all in.* Hmn. Interesting.

TERRY: How are you going to get Springsteen to agree there, big fella?

CHARLES: Why wouldn't he?

BILL and TERRY *laugh a bit, smirk.*

CHARLES: Well, you could get someone else to play him.

TERRY: How are you going to get the rights to the songs?

CHARLES: Sure they will want to.

BILL: Yeah?

CHARLES: It's good promotion. Like product placement.

BILL: Yeah, I guess that's one way of looking at it.

TERRY: Does it have to be Bruce Spingsteen?

CHARLES *thinks about it.*

TERRY: Maybe you could have an auction, to see which mega-millionaire super-star would be willing to pay the most to have the privilege of being some prop in your cruddy movie?

BILL: Come on, Terry.

CHARLES *looks down at his shoes.*

TERRY: Would probably take you five years just to find someone who could get thirty seconds in front of Springsteen's agent to make the pitch.

FROM OFFSTAGE: One man's meat…

JACOB: Another man's poison.

TERRY: If he's not dead by then.

BILL *(to Charles)*: I thought it was interesting.

Connie and Jenny enter the room from stage right and sit with Charles on the couch.

CONNIE: What's up, gents?

JENNY *(smiling, to Charles)*: Hey.

FROM OFFSTAGE: Don't throw the baby out…

JACOB: With the bathwater.

CONNIE: I always thought it was 'with the bath' (?)

TERRY: Bathwater. *(emphasizing 'water')*

BILL: Charles was just telling us about his idea for a screenplay.

JENNY *asks Charles*: what's that? *as CONNIE says:* Oh, that sounds interesting.

TERRY: No, it wasn't.

BILL: Yes it was.

CHARLES *(to Jenny)*: It's stupid. *(shrugging off)*

TERRY: So what do you do when you're not writing blockbuster movies there Chaz?

CHARLES: Uh, well right now I am working at a think tank.

CONNIE: Ooo, that's interesting.

FROM OFFSTAGE: The number of red stripes on an American flag…

JACOB: Thirteen.

FROM OFFSTAGE: Seven.

JACOB: Oh, it's just the red. Stupid. *(hitting forehead with palm of his hand)*

JENNY *(to Charles)*: So tell them what you are doing?

CHARLES: Well, right now we are attempting to evaluate pilot programs to retrofit low-income housing in ways that improve energy efficiency.

TERRY: Who pays you to do that?

CHARLES: Well, we are a non-profit that's primarily funded through foundations like the Ford Foundation and the Bill & Melinda Gates Foundation.

TERRY *rolls his eyes.*

BILL: So what do your parents do, Charles?

CHARLES: My mom runs a bookstore –

TERRY: Does she own the bookstore?

CHARLES: No, uh, she's the man-

TERRY: Then she doesn't run it. The owner runs it.

CHARLES: Uh... well... okay.... - and my dad is a PhD.

CONNIE: Interesting. In what?

FROM OFFSTAGE: "It's not true I had nothing on; I had the radio on"

JACOB: Marilyn Monroe

CHARLES: Um, he's a professor, at Rutgers. In anthropology.

BILL: So does he like dig up old bones and broken necklaces? or pottery?

CHARLES: No, um, he's primarily a linguist.

JENNY: So could he like be an expert in a criminal case where he identifies who the killer is by the way he speaks or the patterns in his e-mails and ransom notes?

CHARLES: Uh. Not, not really. His specialty is the development of prehistoric languages in northwest China and Mongolia.

JENNY *(a bit deflatedly)*: Oh.

FROM OFFSTAGE: The Persistence of Memory by Dali is a example of...

JACOB: Surrealism.

TERRY: That's how they captured the Unabomber you know.

BILL: Can you imagine spending your whole life studying prehistoric languages in northwest China and Mongolia? *(to Charles)* I mean, no offense. Just seems crazy.

JACOB: Sur-real.

JENNY: It's like the guy who guards the rhinoceros.

CONNIE: What?

JENNY: In Zambia, or wherever. Like twenty-four hours a day. Seven days a week. To make sure that the Rhinoceros survives.

CONNIE: Is it made of gold or something?

JENNY: No, like, the species. For future generations.

CONNIE: Ahh.

BILL: And all the time he's probably both relieved that no one is coming, and yet there is also this little part of him hoping and wishing that a poacher would finally come. To fight off. Or else what was the whole point.

CHARLES: Well, better safe than sorry.

JENNY: And in the poacher case, maybe, probably, you were a deterrent. Maybe there would have been a poacher. But you scared him off. So that's what it was for. But what about like a firewatcher? They wait their whole life for the fire. But they aren't actually preventing it.

FROM OFFSTAGE: From a 1920 play by Karel Capek about mechanical men and women...

JACOB: Robot

CHARLES: I guess he is preventing it from getting worse.

JENNY: True. Maybe.

BILL: At least the guy guarding the rhinoceros knows whether he succeeded. You could spend your whole life being the world's foremost expert on what may or may not have been authentic first century Egyptian papyrus. And but then, when you are lying on your deathbed, you don't even really know whether you were actually right about anything you ever thought or said.

OFFSTAGE, a phone rings.

CONNIE *(looking to Bill)*: That's your phone. Maybe that's them. *(as she rises, and BILL also gets up, and they exit, stage right)*

The cellphone stops ringing, and, off-stage, BILL says: Hello.

TERRY *(to Charles)*: What are you so nervous about?

CHARLES: Nothing.

TERRY: You look nervous.

JENNY: He's fine. Leave him alone.

TERRY: Did you knock her up?

CHARLES *laughs, as* JENNY *says*: No!

TERRY: If you knocked her up, you should get an abortion.

JENNY: Grampa, can you please tell your friend to shut up.

FROM OFFSTAGE: Neither shall there be any more a this to destroy the Earth...

JACOB: Shut-up Terry. A flood.

CHARLES *(to Terry)*: Actually didn't peg you as pro-choice?

TERRY: I'm not pro-choice.

JENNY: You're not?

TERRY: No, I'm pro-abortion. We have too many people in this world. The more abortions, the better.

JENNY: That's disgusting.

CHARLES: Actually has a point.

JENNY looks at Charles reproachfully.

FROM OFFSTAGE: Detroit native whose rap album I Decided debuted at Number One on the Billboard charts in 2017...

JACOB: Jay-Z?

CHARLES: Uh, I think it's Big Sean.

Bill and Connie come back onto to the stage.

JENNY: Any news?

Bill resumes his seat in one of the chairs and Connie hers, with Charles and Jenny, on the couch.

CONNIE: Nope. Not yet. *(and after a brief pause)* Was just Ralph calling.

JENNY: Not big fan of rap, Granpa?

TERRY: Nobody is. They are just afraid to say it stinks because they're worried people will call them a racist.

JENNY: Maybe some people don't like it because they are racists.

TERRY: I don't see color.

CHARLES: Think it's a generational thing.

BILL: Like comedy.

CHARLES: Exactly.

BILL *(to Terry)*: So when you see a black person, does he look like a white person, or is he invisible?

TERRY: His skin looks white. But he's dressed either a lot worse or a lot better.

FROM OFFSTAGE: This Emily Brontë novel was the inspiration for a Kate Bush song...

JACOB: Wuthering Heights

JENNY *(to Charles)*: Have you ever read that book, Wuthering Heights?

CHARLES: Not that I remember.

TERRY: I thought you wanted to be a great writer?

CHARLES: Well, maybe so. But I never said I wanted to be a great reader.

JENNY: Why don't you just tell us what are you guys waiting to hear?

CONNIE: Something to do with dad's work.

JENNY: Is it bad?

BILL: No, it's not bad.

TERRY *(to Jacob)*: He's building to the big reveal.

BILL: Shut-up Terry.

TERRY *(turning to Bill)*: Just level with them.

BILL: Shut-up, Terry.

CONNIE *says*: What is he talking about? *as* JENNY *says:* Level with us about what?

TERRY: Just tell them.

BILL: Shut up, Terry.

JENNY: Tell us what?

TERRY: They are going to find out eventually.

CONNIE: Bill?

BILL: It's not just whether I get the promotion. *(to Jenny)* If I get this promotion, we have to re-locate, sweetie. It's a good promotion; will be making a lot more money; but we would have to move. *(and to Connie)* And if I don't get the promotion, I'll be out of a job.

CONNIE: What ?!?!

TERRY: There it is: the big reveal....

BILL: Yep. *(Connie looks at him incredulously)* It's all or nothing.

Scene Three.

A child/teenager's bedroom. Charles is lying on his back on the bed, made up with a colorfully woven blanket or duvet. Jenny is lying on her back on the floor, atop a simple rug. Plain. Inexpensive. Grey or beige. Behind and over the bed, on the wall, are some museum posters, (maybe Renoir's Boating Party, or Turner's Venice, or something by Georgia O'Keeffe), as well as a concert or movie poster or two, (maybe Eminem or late U2, Bend it Like Beckham or Million Dollar Baby). Next to the bed is a bookshelf. Charles is flipping through paperbacks. Jenny is twirling a necklace over her head.

JENNY: I'm sorry.

CHARLES: Sorry for what?

JENNY: For bringing you here, -

CHARLES: Don't be silly.

JENNY: Exposing you to this.

CHARLES: "Every family is unhappy in its own way."

JENNY: And then the big reveal….

CHARLES: Well you aren't really living at home anymore anyway, are you?

JENNY: Um ….

CHARLES: I mean you will graduate from college and then you'll get a job somewhere; or go to graduate school; or get married?

JENNY: I guess, but I still like having a place to come home to. And what about my parents?

A brief silence.

CHARLES: When it gets right down to it, there are really only a limited number of big reveals.

JENNY: Okay. But what do you think my parents would do if he lost his job?

CHARLES: Either someone cheated on someone. Or someone you didn't think was your mom or dad actually turns out to be your mom or dad. Or someone you thought was your kid turns out not to be your kid. Or someone you thought was dead is really alive. Or someone was abused or molested.

JENNY: Or had an abortion.

CHARLES: Like Uncle Terry?

JENNY: That was crazy.

CHARLES: I think he had a point.

JENNY: No he didn't.

CHARLES: It's like that One Child policy in China. If it happened to you, it would suck. But, for the rest of the world, aren't you kinda glad?

JENNY: I know it sounds horrible, but I don't really care. What if my parents move away? Or my dad loses his job? Or if they move away and he loses his job?

CHARLES: Move in with me.

JENNY: Yeah, right?

CHARLES: Why not?

JENNY *doesn't say anything for a time, as Charles waits for an answer.*

CHARLES: O-kay....

JENNY: I'm just not ready.

CHARLES: I get it. Okay.

JENNY: Someone could die.

CHARLES: What?

JENNY: Big reveal. That's something else that could happen. Someone could die.

CHARLES: Yeah, but that's not really a reveal. It's a turning-point, I guess; potentially.

JENNY: What if they have cancer. Or some other untreatable disease. Like Huntington's. That could be a reveal.

CHARLES: So not death, but that you are dying.

JENNY: Or what you thought was an accident was really a suicide.

CHARLES: That's a good one.

JENNY: Or what you thought was a suicide was really something else.

CHARLES: It's usually not even a big reveal, when push comes to shove. It's small. It just feels big.

JENNY: That's because you're being objective about it. People who are trapped within their own subjective realities don't see things that way.

She makes a grimace and scratches an itch on the side of her face. And then adds:

We experience them as the melodramas we have come to expect from movies and school, or tv.

CHARLES *keeps flipping thru a paperback, without saying anything.*

JENNY: When do you need to head back?

CHARLES: Probably around 10:00.

JENNY: Can have breakfast.

CHARLES: That'll be warm and fuzzy.

JENNY: Shut-up.

CHARLES: Are you going to feel weird sleeping in the same room in your parents' house?

JENNY: No.

CHARLES: Are your parents?

JENNY: I don't know. Don't think so. Not my mom anyway.

CHARLES: Grandpa?

JENNY: No. He's cool.

CHARLES: So out of it.

JENNY: No he's not.

CHARLES: Did you tell your parents about the ticket?

JENNY: No.

CHARLES: Why were you even going that way? You know it's a speed trap.

JENNY: I don't know. Can't help it. Like ninety percent of my driving is by habit.

CHARLES: Maybe your mom or dad knows someone who can fix it?

JENNY: I guess; maybe.

CHARLES: What do you think is the best movie of the 1990s?

JENNY: Kind of an odd segue.

CHARLES: Were fighting about it at work the other day.

JENNY: Did you win?

CHARLES: Maybe.

JENNY: Seldom that anyone actually changes his or her mind about things.

CHARLES: Is that the measure?

JENNY: What else?

CHARLES: Good point. *(a brief pause)* So what was the best movie of the 1990s?

JENNY: The best or my favorite?

CHARLES: You do that too?

JENNY: Of course.

CHARLES: That's why we're perfect for each other.

And, after a brief silence:

JENNY: So how do we compare to your other girlfriends' families?

CHARLES: A hundred percent average?

JENNY: Come on. Really. Aren't we more dysfunctional?

CHARLES: Heck no.

JENNY: So give me an example.

CHARLES: Well I had this girlfriend in high school. Margaret. I think I've mentioned her. And her parents were really flaky. They were always fighting. And the brother was on drugs. Think the parents eventually split up. She always thought her mom was cheating on her dad.

JENNY: Was she?

CHARLES: I don't know. She was flaky. But....

JENNY: What about Claire's family?

CHARLES: I don't want to talk about that.

JENNY: Why not?

CHARLES: Just don't.

JENNY: Some big secret?

CHARLES: No.

A pause.

JENNY: Just special?

CHARLES: No.

JENNY: You have to protect her (?)

CHARLES: No.

JENNY: Defend her.

CHARLES: No. Jeez. It's not that big of a deal.

JENNY: It is to me.

CHARLES: Why?

JENNY: Because you shouldn't have any secrets from me.

CHARLES: So if you tell me something, now, in confidence, and in twenty years I am married to someone else, I should tell her your secret?

JENNY: Why would you be with someone else?

CHARLES: I'm just saying 'if'.

JENNY *stands and goes to the edge of the bed, looking off-stage. (as thru a window)*

CHARLES: Now you're mad at me.

JENNY *still doesn't say anything.*

CHARLES: C-o-m-e – o-n, *(as he stands and puts his arms around her waist).*

JENNY: It's fine. It is what it is. *(still looking away)* You'll always love Claire.

CHARLES: No, I won't. I don't even like Claire. I love you.

JENNY: If you say so.

CHARLES: I do, *(and, with his arms still around her waist, kisses her cheek).*

JENNY *(non-committal)*: I love you too.

> *She turns, and they kiss on the lips, and separate.*
>
> *Charles sits on the bed, and Jenny sits on the bed beside him.*

CHARLES: Your parents don't like me, do they?

JENNY: Yes they do.

CHARLES: Nah, I can tell.

JENNY: Who cares if they like you.

CHARLES: So they don't.

JENNY: That's not what I said. I just said that, whether they do or not, who cares? I don't care if your parents like me.

CHARLES: My parents love you.

JENNY: Well, maybe they shouldn't.

CHARLES: Why not?

JENNY *shrugs.*

CHARLES: Why shouldn't they love you?

JENNY: I'm not Claire.

CHARLES: If it's any consolation, they hated Claire.

JENNY: That's why you still love her.

CHARLES: No I don't.

JENNY: Forbidden fruit.

CHARLES: More like rotten fruit.

JENNY: Like … banana? Or like mango?

CHARLES: Uh, like … pineapple?

JENNY: Gross.

A brief silence.

CHARLES: You never did answer my question.

JENNY: What question?

CHARLES: The one I asked you before.

JENNY: Best movie of the Nineties?

CHARLES: No. If you tell me a secret, don't you expect me to keep it? No matter what?

JENNY *(annoyed)*: I don't know. I thought we were past that. Why do you want to bring that up again?

CHARLES: I'm sorry.

JENNY: It's like you just want to win some kind of intellectual contest or something.

CHARLES: I'm sorry.

JENNY: I'm not as smart as you.

CHARLES: That's not true.

JENNY: Okay? Is that what you want to hear?

CHARLES: No. That's not true. You're much smarter than me.

JENNY: Whatever.

CHARLES: That's not what I'm saying.

JENNY: Then what are you saying?

CHARLES: I don't know. I don't even know what we are fighting about.

CONNIE (from Off-Stage): J-E-N-N-Y !

JENNY: C-O-M-I-N-G ! *(and then to Charles)* Yes, you do.

Scene Four

Living Room. Jacob in la-z-boy, Terry in chair, Bill and Charles on the couch. They are watching what is presumably a television off-stage where the audience is sitting. Bill is sipping whiskey from a glass.

JACOB: So this one day I was driving down the road and I pick up this hitch-hiker. 'Thanks for picking me up' he says. 'Everyone's afraid that you might be a serial killer.' 'No problem' I said. 'The odds of having two serial killers in one car together are extremely unlikely.'

CHARLES *nods to Jacob and laughs.*

TERRY *(to Charles)*: You smoke?

CHARLES: No.

TERRY: Not even pot?

CHARLES: Uh, no.

BILL: Never?

CHARLES: Well, you know, I've tried it. But, like President Clinton, I didn't inhale.

BILL: Right.

CHARLES: I have just always found the notion of smoking something, anything, just viscerally disgusting.

TERRY: That's not what he said.

And, after a brief silence:

CHARLES: You know what I hate even?

BILL: What?

CHARLES: When someone even goes outside to smoke, but when they come back inside they still have it in their lungs and they breath the smoke back out.

BILL: Hmn.

and taking another sip

CHARLES: Did you ever smoke?

BILL: For a little while. When Jenny came along I quit.

CHARLES: Was it difficult?

BILL: I don't really remember.

JACOB: So, I read a guide to marriage counselling, and they said you should treat your wife the way you did on your very first date. So after dinner tonight, I think I'll drop her back off at her parents' house.

CHARLES *laughs again.* Good one.

JENNY *comes into the room with a tray of cheese and crackers.*

CHARLES: Thanks, babe.

JENNY: 'Babe'?

CHARLES: Sorry.

JENNY: So how's it going?

BILL: Oh, shit.

JENNY: What?

BILL: Nothing.

JENNY: Okay, well, I'll leave you to it.

> *and after putting the tray down on the coffee table in front of the couch turns and leaves the room, off-stage, presumably back into the kitchen*

TERRY *coughs.*

BILL: You okay?

TERRY: Fine.

CHARLES: You want any cheese and crackers?

TERRY, *still coughing a bit, shakes his head 'No'.*

JACOB: A man asks his wife, 'what would you do if I won the lottery?' She said 'I would take my half and leave you.' 'Great' he said. 'I won twelve dollars. Here's a five and a one. Keep in touch.'

CHARLES *nods to Jacob and laughs.*

BILL: Where do you think the bird goes when it storms?

CHARLES *looks over at him. Doesn't say anything.*

TERRY *(to Bill)*: Still haven't heard anything, huh?

BILL: No.

TERRY: You can't teach hungry.

BILL: Well, then, how can you learn it?

CHARLES, *while eating a cracker with cheese on it, nods his head to something on the television.*

TERRY: Is that one of your rap stars?

CHARLES: Well, hip-hop.

TERRY: What's the difference?

CHARLES: I think rap is a sub-set of hip-hop.

BILL: Hmn. *(and takes another sip)*

TERRY: Remember when everyone was a one-hit wonder, and then his name would become synonymous with that one song?

BILL: Like Oliver 'Who Shot the LaLa' Morgan?

TERRY: Yeah, Oliver 'Who Shot the LaLa' Morgan... Robert 'Barefootin' Parker... Al 'Carnival Time' Johnson... Jessie 'Oo Poo Pah Do' Hill.

CHARLES: What about that Big Bopper guy?

BILL: I think he just was the Big Bopper. I don't think he had a song called 'The Big Bopper'.

TERRY: No, his big hit was....

CHARLES: What about Chubby Checker?

BILL: Who do you think came first: Chubby Checker, or Fats Domino?

TERRY: Chantilly Lace.

CHARLES: I think you'd be Chubby first, and then you would work your way up to Fat.

BILL: Or maybe Fats is the original, and Chubby is just a cheap knock-off. Like a chip off the real block.

JACOB: So this man escapes from a prison where he's been locked up for fifteen years. He breaks into a house and finds a young couple in bed. He orders the guy to get out of bed and ties him to a chair. Then he ties his wife to the bed, kisses her neck, and then goes into the bathroom. The husband whispers to his wife, 'I'm sorry, honey. But this guy seems very dangerous. If he gets angry, he'll kill us both. So don't resist, don't complain... do whatever he tells you. Be strong, honey. I love you!' 'He wasn't kissing my neck' the wife says. 'He told me that he's gay, thinks you're cute, and asked if we had any Vaseline. I told him it was in the bathroom. Be strong, honey. I love you too.'

CHARLES *nods to Jacob and laughs, and then looks back to the off-stage television screen. He takes another cracker.*

TERRY *(also watching)*: Can anyone figure out what is going on?

CHARLES: I think they are talking about AI.

BILL: That's not AI.

TERRY: Nope.

BILL: There's no I at all, don't think. Just A.

CHARLES *chuckles.*

TERRY: It's man versus machine. More men. More machines. Less jobs.

CHARLES: I think it's in many ways actually complimentary.

TERRY: Tell that to John Henry.

BILL *(raising his glass)*: To John Henry.

TERRY: Or even Brother Bill there. Waiting by the phone.... The big reveal....

BILL: Thank you for your concern, Terry.

TERRY *nods a 'you're welcome'.*

BILL: Got nothing to do with it.

TERRY: Diversity hire?

BILL: No.

JACOB: Which letter is silent in 'scent', the S or the C?

TERRY: I don't think anyone really cares about diversity. I think it's just an angle.

CHARLES: Respectfully, I don't agree with that. I think plenty of people think diversity is important.

TERRY: If it helps them get what they want.

CHARLES: No, I think people recognize that it's important to bring different perspectives into the fold, to allow for better decision-making. Eliminate blind spots. Reflect better the people you are serving, or selling to, as partners, or customers, so they have a comfort and a confidence that they are being treated fairly. And all of those things bring value to an organization. In addition to recognizing the fact that people start out on different playing fields; that the measures and markers of talent or success are inherently skewed and subjective; and to try to make up for some of the inequities and indignities of the past.

TERRY *(to Bill)*: You got a smooth talker here. Think Jenny should hold onto this one. He could sell sand to an Arab in the desert.

BILL *raises his glass.*

TERRY *(now to Charles)*:   But let me ask you something, big honcho: Does that mean, when the time comes, you are going to step aside?

CHARLES: What do you mean?

TERRY *(to Bill)*: You see? *(and back to Charles)* Everything is all well and good when you are talking about someone else's seat. But when you are willing to give up your own seat, then I'll maybe take you seriously.

BILL: Leave him alone, Terry. This has nothing to do with you. And it really has nothing to do with me.

TERRY: So what is it, age?

BILL: No.

TERRY: They putting you out to pasture?

BILL: No one is putting me anywhere. I am getting a promotion. Everything is gonna be fine. *(takes a small sip)* Better than fine.

JACOB: When a poison expires, does that mean it's no longer poisonous? or even more poisonous?

TERRY: They just use it to bully you. If you don't do what they want you to do for them, you're a sexist. If you don't say what they want, you're a racist.

BILL: Everybody bullies. Terry. Everybody wants what they want. No one is immune from being a victim or a perpetrator. Everyone's got it in em. Like angels and devils. Some get luckier or unluckier depending on the time and the place and the circumstances. But we all grab for whatever weapons seem closest at hand.

Scene Five

Kitchen. Bill, Connie, Jenny and Charles around the breakfast table. There is a nice roast in the center of the table, with potatoes and asparagus. Each has a wine and a water glass, but Bill also has a glass of whiskey. While he is a bit tipsy, the atmosphere seems for the most part light and jovial. They are eating and drinking and laughing over dinner.

BILL: I'll bet you dollars to donuts….

JENNY: So which is it, daddy? Do you want the dollars or do you want the donuts?

BILL: Well, since I'm right, I guess I will take both.

CONNIE: Gosh I sure wish they would call.

BILL: Sure everything will be fine.

JENNY: No news is good news, right?

BILL: Yep.

CONNIE: Maybe, if they do let you go, you should file an age discrimination case?

CHARLES: Kick ass, Mr. Hamm. Take names. Take prisoners.

JENNY: Can you do that?

BILL: I don't know.

CHARLES: Is it take prisoners, or don't take prisoners?

BILL: It's don't take prisoners.

CHARLES: Why don't you want to take prisoners?

BILL: They shoot them.

CHARLES: Ouch.

JENNY: I mean, I understand for women and minorities, being able to sue. But why old white men?

BILL *says*: Uh, I'm not that old, yet, *as CONNIE says*: Because that's the law.

JENNY: Not fair.

CHARLES: Why not?

JENNY: Because that's the way it's been for thousands of years. It's always been the old white men running everything. Why do they need to be protected?

BILL: I'm just doing the best I can, Jenny. *(and he takes a big swig)* I only have one life. Just doing the best I can with it.

CONNIE: You think those corporations care about race and gender and color? They don't care about that. And they don't care about the last two thousand years. What they care about is money.

JENNY: But –

CONNIE: People, like your father, slave away loyally for decades. And for what? To save jobs? To lower prices? No, of course not. For executive stock options. And buy-backs. And CEO bonuses.

JENNY: But what's that got to do with discrimination?

CONNIE: They don't want them to get their pensions, *(with an emphasis on 'don't' and 'pensions'),* honey.

JENNY: Or maybe they just want to give new opportunities to younger women, and people of color.

BILL *takes another swig of whiskey.*

JENNY: You can't just rest on your privilege and assume that you'll be taken care of.

CONNIE: Spoken like someone who's never had to go out and work for a living.

CHARLES: There are plenty of poor white men, hon.

BILL *(slamming his whiskey glass on the table)*: This has nothing to do with it. It's nothing to do with diversity, or age discrimination, or privilege. It's just me. It's just business. They either want me, or they don't.

JENNY: Yeah, it doesn't have anything to do with diversity because you guys don't have any women or people of color at that place. Except maybe the secretaries.

BILL: So what should I do, Jenny? Just crawl into a hole? Step aside, and give up? Not try?

JENNY *(after a brief pause, looking down at the table)*: No, daddy.

CONNIE: God knows that everyone admires those spoiled little manchilds who just sit around and go to galas, sopping up their family fortunes and not even trying to ever make something of their lives.

JENNY *smiles, trying to ease the tension.*

CHARLES: Remember: *(and lifting his wine glass)* 'Women who seek to be equal with men lack ambition.'

Everyone laughs, except Bill.

CONNIE: And men who seek to be equal with women lack ... whatever is the opposite of naivety.

Which Jenny in particular appreciates.

BILL: So, Chaz, if I may call you that –

CHARLES: Of course.

BILL: – when did you realize that you wanted to be a tank thinker?

CHARLES: I'm not sure that was ever really my dream.

BILL: No?

CHARLES: Or even a plan.

BILL: Headhunter, came and picked you out of the undulating throng?

CHARLES *(laughing politely)*: Not really.

BILL: No?

CHARLES: Well, my dad has this friend....

JENNY: It's very hard for kids just out of college these days, dad.

BILL *(dryly)*: I'm sure.

JENNY: Remember Cynthia Rodgers?

BILL *says* No, *while* CONNIE *says*: Of course.

JENNY: She graduated with a 3.6 from Cornell and had to take a job as a barista.

CHARLES: And $175,000 in loans to repay.

BILL: You have loans there, Charles?

CHARLES: Not too bad.

JENNY: But you don't have to start paying back for a few years, right?

CHARLES: Yep.

BILL: But the interest clock is still ticking.

CONNIE *(to Charles)*: So tell us about the bookstore. That must be a nice place.

CHARLES: Yeah, so it's like this old Victorian mansion from the 1800s that was converted into an art gallery in the 1960s, and then ….

BILL stands up while Charles is still talking.

CHARLES: …. um, in the early Eighties, … that's ….

CONNIE *(to Bill)*: Can I get you something?

Bill starts to walk over to the liquor cabinet and a spotlight follows him. The lights fade over Connie, Jenny and Charles at the dinner table. Bill pours a glass of whiskey, and stands there for a minute. Wipes his brow. Takes another sip. The spotlight follows him back to the table, and starts to recede, as the dinner table lights come back up. Bill takes his seat again as Charles is speaking to Connie...

CHARLES: …. and the reason why my dad is so interested in Giglamesh is that we know Gilgamesh only from itself. We don't really have any other writings to place it into context or know really anything about the world in which it was written. And so the translations, my dad says, are just basically English, that's loosely stapled to a broken set of ancient pottery. *(laughs to himself)* I mean, that's him talking; I ….

BILL: Who the fuck is Gilgamesh?

Silence.

CHARLES: Most people think he was a King of Uruk, in arou-

BILL *raises his hand to Charles, signaling 'stop'*: I know.

And, after a pause,

CONNIE *(to Bill)*: What is wrong with you?

BILL: Nothing.

CONNIE: I know you are under a lot of stress, but we are all under a lot of stress.

BILL: I'm not under stress. *(and takes a sip)* Unstressed. Laid back. Hanging ten. Is that what it is?

JENNY: Yes. Dork.

BILL: Hanging fifteen.

CONNIE: Don't you think it's strange that you still haven't heard yet?

BILL *does not reply.*

CHARLES: Don't you think it's so interesting and ironic that that part of the world, Iran, Iraq, all of these backwards countries, are really the Cradle of Civilization?

JENNY *shoots him a glare.*

CONNIE: That is funny.

BILL: Not 'hah hah' funny though.

CONNIE: What is wrong with you?

JENNY *(to Charles)*: I'm sorry. I shouldn't have invited you.

CHARLES: No, it's okay.

CONNIE *(to Charles)*: It's just a stressful time for us.

BILL: It's not a stressful time.

JENNY: No, you're just an asshole.

CONNIE: Jennifer!

CHARLES: Really, it's okay. It's a bad time. I can go.

BILL: It's not a bad time, Charles. It's not a stressful time. It's the endless time of the ocean that waves and ebbs and strays – and sprays, while we try to come to terms with it; and whatever you think; whatever talents or wisdoms or skills we think we have when we are, what are you? – twenty-four? –

CHARLES *nods his head.*

BILL: – the insights and the intelligence we think we have collected won't protect you from the storm that's coming. When they put a gun to your head *(forming one with his thumb and index finger)* – or her head *(Jenny's)* – with blood under his fingernails and hurricane eyes –

CONNIE: Bill!

BILL *(almost whispering)*: Or the scarier, more profound and slumbering underbrush of uncertainty and procrastination, seeping, wickedly silent, where resentment meets indifference. … Without purpose. … Encroaching like a cancerous dark esophagus into the seeds of doubt and self-questioning; and cowardice; and every bit of happy life goes plunging on around you…. And who knows if you will be there for her when *(searching for the words)* …. Or if she will be there for you.

JENNY: But I will though.

BILL: I know you think that, and maybe you will. Lots of people do. *(and then turning to Charles)* And lots of people don't.

CHARLES: Sir, I respect you sir. But you don't know me.

CONNIE *pleads* That's not what he's saying, *as* BILL *says*: No, I don't.

JENNY: You're so unfair, daddy? You're so mean. Chaz never did anything to you. Or mom. Or me, that was bad.

CONNIE: It's just that you're young. That's all dad is saying.

JENNY: Only two years younger than you were.

CONNIE: Well….

JENNY: So it was a mistake?

CONNIE: No!

JENNY: Is that what you mean?

CONNIE: No! Of course not.

JENNY: I was just a mistake.

CONNIE: Don't be silly.

JENNY: That's what you said!

CONNIE: That's not what I said.

BILL: You'll see. When you have kids.

JENNY: Not according to you. If you and mom get your way I'll never get married, and never have kids.

CONNIE: Of course we want you to get married and have children.

JENNY: Just not til I'm thirty.

CHARLES: Maybe I should just go.

BILL: Okay.

JENNY *says* No, Daddy, *while CONNIE says:* No, Bill! No. *(and to Charles)* Sit down, Charles. This has gotten out of hand. It's a very stressful time. We are happy that you have come into Jenny's life. And if it's your intention to propose –

CHARLES: Propose!?! *(and to Jenny)* Hey, I like you a lot, maybe even love you – I mean I know I say I love you – but I wasn't planning to propose.

JENNY: You're not?

CHARLES: Well maybe eventually. But....

JENNY *runs offstage crying.*

CONNIE *follows.*

Bill takes a sip of whisky.

And, after a minute:

CHARLES: You think I should wait and ... (?)

A telephone rings. Bill takes another sip.

CHARLES *(starting to stand)*: Maybe I should just go

The phone continues to ring.

CHARLES *(now standing)*: I'm very sorry sir. I didn't mean to brush up things.

The phone continues to ring.

CHARLES: Aren't you going to get it? That may be the call.

BILL *(standing)*: Remember Charles: The yellow cardinal dies alone.

The phone continues to ring, as Bill walks offstage, leaving Charles alone, standing, beside the table, as the lights come down.

BILL *(from Off-Stage)*: Hello?

ACT TWO

Scene One.

Living Room. Jacob on the recliner, Jenny on the couch.

FROM OFFSTAGE: Girl with a Pearl Earring is the story of Griet, who works in the household of this Seventeenth Century painter.

JACOB: Vermeer

FROM OFFSTAGE: "Share moments, share life" with what company's products?

JACOB: Kodak

FROM OFFSTAGE: Willy Loman and his son, Biff.

JACOB: Death of a Salesman. *(and then, to Jenny)* Is Kodak even in business still? I thought they went bankrupt.

JENNY *does not respond.*

FROM OFFSTAGE: "Computers are useless. They can only give you answers"

JACOB: Um, … Freud, maybe?

FROM OFFSTAGE: Picasso

> *Jacob looks over to Jenny, who is pensive.*

JACOB: Hey, *(he says to Jenny),* did you hear about the man who sued the hospital because his wife lost interest in sex after surgery?

JENNY: What?

JACOB: It was cataract surgery.

JENNY: That's funny.

JACOB: A few years ago, Terry's wife was complaining that he never bought her flowers. So I asked Terry about it, and he said, 'I never knew she sold flowers'.

JENNY: That sounds like Terry.

FROM OFFSTAGE: "In Reading Gaol by Reading Town there is a pit of shame..."

JACOB: D.H. Lawrence.

FROM OFFSTAGE: Oscar Wilde.

JACOB *(to Jenny)*: Did you know that? Oscar Wilde?

JENNY *shakes her head 'No'.*

JACOB: So what's been dragging you so down around the mouth?

JENNY: Nothing.

JACOB: Is it that boy?

JENNY: Charles.

JACOB: Yes, I know. Nice boy.

JENNY: Did you really like him?

JACOB: Sure.

JENNY: But?

JACOB: Sweetie, whether I like him or not doesn't matter. I did. But whatever makes you happy makes me happy.

JENNY *smiles.*

JACOB: So what happened?

JENNY: I'm too young. He's too old. My parents. His family.

JACOB: All the usual.

JENNY: I know. Everything's a cliché until it happens to you.

JACOB: That's how it becomes a cliché in the first place.

JENNY: I just wish….

    After a silence:

JACOB: I wish your grandmother was here, to see you.

JENNY *brightens a bit.*

JACOB: She used to call you her little hummingbird. So fast and fluttering here and there, on tiny gusts of energy.

JENNY: I remember this smell….

JACOB: Probably anise.

JENNY: Anise?

JACOB: Like licorice. Or Thai Tea?

JENNY: Yeah, not licorice.

JACOB: When you were a baby, she – and your mom – would boil anise stars with a little sugar. Let it cool. And then give it to you warm in a bottle. It would settle your tummy.

JENNY: Yeah, mom would tell me about that. But that's not what I smell.

JACOB: It's 'nectar'.

JENNY: Yes!

JACOB: That's what she called it. Honey Tea.

JENNY: With cream.

JACOB: Sweet cream.

JENNY: And that's Thai Tea? *(with an emphasis on* **'Thai'***)*

JACOB: Approximately.

JENNY: They've all gone to paper straws now. I guess the plastic is bad for the environment. But the paper ones kind of disintegrate.

JACOB: In Native American lore, two siblings are left alone while their parents go off to find food during a time of famine. The little boy carves a piece of wood into a small bird in order to entertain his sister. She takes the carving, and tosses it into the air, and, magically, it comes to life – turning into a hummingbird. Who flies off to the God of Fertility, to ask for rain. The skies begin to open, and the crops begin to grow again.

JENNY *looks to Jacob warmly.*

JACOB: In Aztec culture, though, the hummingbird was a symbol of war. Isn't that crazy?

JENNY: Weird.

FROM OFFSTAGE: Around 1507, this Polish astronomer began trying to prove that the Sun, not the Earth, was the center of the Universe.

JACOB: Copernicus

JENNY: Polish?

JACOB: That's what they tell us.

JENNY: Doesn't sound Polish.

JACOB: What does it sound like?

JENNY: I don't know. Never really thought about it. Italian maybe. Greek?

Bill enters. He is wearing a three-piece suit and tie.

JACOB: How did it go?

Jenny stands up and leaves the room (i.e. the stage).

Bill follows her quietly with his eyes.

JACOB *(to Bill)*: One good thing:

BILL: What's that?

JACOB: You get to say 'I told you so'.

BILL: Somehow that's never satisfying for quite as long as you expect it to be.

JACOB: How did the interview go?

BILL: Alright, I guess.

JACOB: You'll know when they call you to tell you whether or not you got the job.

BILL: Yep.

JACOB: People always want to know the answer before they begin. When you get to the end, I tell them, then you'll know what the right answer was.

BILL: You know, while Connie's not in the room, I can tell you: I specifically made coffee early this morning so that things would start moving and I could get something out before the interview. But it didn't work, and now my insides are a mess. *(and after a pause)* Too much information?

JACOB: No, it's just information that I'm not very interested in.

BILL: Fair response.

JACOB: Do you need to excuse yourself?

BILL: No, I just want to sit for a minute.

JACOB: So your daughter is pretty broken up about you breaking her up.

BILL: I didn't break them up.

JACOB: No?

BILL: I just prematurely exposed the cracks and fissures that would have developed over time so they could see them before it was too late.

JACOB: Cracks in her, or cracks in you?

BILL: Cracks in Chaz. *(drawing out 'Chaz')*

JACOB: I don't think Jennie sees the cracks in him that you do.

BILL: To the artist in love, the face is merely a suggestion of what the portrait might be.

JACOB: To the mechanic in love also.

BILL *smiles.*

JACOB: Or the gravedigger.   Or the window clerk.
Or the m-

BILL: He's a washer.

JACOB: What?

BILL: Charles. He's a washer.

JACOB: What's that mean?

BILL: There are nuts. There are bolts. And there are
washers. He is a washer.

TERRY *enters the room.*

JACOB *(to Bill)*: As I said, you don't always know
the right answer until you get to the end. *(and then to
Terry)* Hello, Terry.

BILL: Maybe they don't want to know.

TERRY: Afternoon, fellas. *(and then to Bill)* Want to
know what?

> *as he sits on the couch*

BILL: Emma's Riddle

TERRY: Whatever that means.   *(and then)*   Find a
job, yet?

BILL: No, not yet.

TERRY: Did they ever give you a reason?

BILL: What?

TERRY: For giving you the ouster.

BILL: Not really.

JACOB: He was too drunk to remember.

BILL: No I wasn't.

TERRY: Too bad about Jenny's friend.

BILL *looks at him quizzically.*

TERRY: I really liked that young feller.

BILL: You're joking, right?

TERRY: No, I fancied him.

JACOB *repeats* 'fancied'? *as BILL asks*: Why?

TERRY: He just seems to have that youthful wide-eyed touch of enthusiasm, and forward-looking, unbridled undaunted unjaded and undeterred naivety.

BILL *(to Jacob)*: He's like a thesaurus.

JACOB: Must have been playing BINGO at the Senior Center.

TERRY: F* You.

JENNY *comes back into the room and sits in one of the armchairs.*

JACOB: Okay, Okay, the show is coming back on.

TERRY: What's with all these Modelo ads all of the sudden? Since 1925? Never heard of it.

JENNY: Lots of college kids drink it.

FROM OFFSTAGE: When asked about insider trading charges, she said "I just want to focus on my salad"

JACOB: Martha Stewart

BILL: What do you and your friends like better, Modelo or Corona?

JENNY: Corona

TERRY: Same lunch-pailer pissing in both.

JENNY *says* You're disgusting, *while BILL laughs a bit, shaking his head and burying his eyes in his hands.*

TERRY: Do you think Martha Stewart should have gone to jail?

JENNY: She lied to the FBI. *(with an emphasis on 'lied')*

FROM OFFSTAGE: In 1941, this Jezebel actress became the first woman to serve as head of the Motion Picture Academy.

JACOB: Bette Davis

TERRY: So why can't you lie to the FBI? They can lie to you.

BILL: I thought she went to jail for some type of a stock deal (?)

TERRY: It's like in Congress: They put people under oath; but then they sit up there lying their asses off.

JENNY: So it's okay to lie? Just cuz someone else is doing it?

BILL: I don't even think there is anything wrong with the stock deal. I mean she is just sitting at home, minding her own business, and gets a call from someone, telling her to sell. What is she supposed to do? Nothing? She wasn't out there trying to take advantage of the system. She was just sitting at home and got a call.

TERRY: But what about the poor sod who she sold the stock to?

JENNY, *annoyed, stands up again, and leaves the room.*

BILL: I don't think that's how the market works.

FROM OFFSTAGE: Kalki, the tenth and last avatar of this Hindu god, is to wreak havoc, on a white horse, with a blazing sword.

JACOB: Vishnu

TERRY *(to Bill)*: No one bought the stock that she sold?

BILL: Would have bought it anyway. From someone else.

TERRY: Not if they knew what she knew.

BILL: Sucker born every minute.

TERRY: How do you know?

BILL: Think we're proof.

TERRY: Speak for yourself.

BILL: Think we're all proof.

Scene Two.

Kitchen. Connie and Betty sitting at the table with water or Coke Zero or iced tea.

CONNIE: Congratulations on your third 49th Birthday.

> *They raise and tap their glasses.*

BETTY: Remind me, before I leave, to borrow that crock pot from you.

CONNIE: I can't believe that you have to cook on your own birthday.

BETTY: I like cooking.

CONNIE: So do I. But would like it if Bill could take me to a nice restaurant every once in a while.

BETTY: Still rough, huh?

CONNIE: Yeah, we are talking about maybe putting the house up for sale.

BETTY: Oh Connie.

CONNIE: Not the end of the world.

BETTY: I know, but….

CONNIE: And then Jenny is going through this break-up.

BETTY: I thought you were happy about that?

CONNIE scans around the stage with her eyes and puts her finger in front of her lips, signing 'shhhh'.

BETTY: Gotcha.

CONNIE: And what's going on with your family? Is Henry here for your birthday?

BETTY: I don't think so.

CONNIE: When's the last time you saw him?

BETTY: It's been a while. *(she takes a sip from her class – and then a deep breath)* You know, I feel guilty. I really do. But I just think that I need to stay away, for my own preservation.

CONNIE *nods in solidarity.*

BETTY: It's like: When you're in your spaceship, and you see a black hole, you don't go check it out. You steer clear, so you don't get sucked in.

CONNIE: Exactly. I wouldn't feel bad about it. You didn't create his troubles. You have your own life, with your own family, and your own challenges that you have to pull yourself through.

BETTY: I know, rationally, but... Unfortunately doesn't change the way that you experience things.

CONNIE: You know I was watching Bill around my brother one time. And my brother around Bill. Everyone's being so nice, and polite. Quiet. And non-confrontational. Agreeable even, on things you know they don't agree. And it occurred to me that, of everyone you know, you probably have the most distorted picture of your brother-in-law. Probably see them at their fakest.

BETTY: What about spouses?

CONNIE: Yeah, but you have such a wider pallet of experience to draw from.

BETTY: You know.

CONNIE: Exactly.

BETTY: What about Elizabeth's husband?

CONNIE: Yeah, that's a lot of fakery.

BETTY: But she knew, don't you think?   I think she knew.

CONNIE: Who can be certain. It's like…. We try to be sympathetic, in the abstract.   But then when something hits close to home, we kinda blame the victim. Not really cuz of morals. But just because we need to preserve the faith that we have a certain amount of control. And wouldn't have let that happen to you.

BETTY: I don't think I do that.

CONNIE: I think I do.

BETTY: Like when?

CONNIE: I don't know in particular, but if, say, you found out that someone's kid were on drugs. Or got pregnant. Or were expelled. I would probably blame the parents. But am I really doing something so different?

BETTY: No blueprint for telling people how to be a good mother.

CONNIE: More like just trying not to do anything that a bad mother would do.

BETTY: Exactly. And that's hard to define too. It's like obscenity: You know it when you see it.

CONNIE: Did you see that Nate and Anne's kid got arrested? Speaking of.

BETTY: I heard that he wasn't really the target; they wanted him to finger someone else, and he wouldn't.

CONNIE: That's crazy.

BETTY: Yeah, but we don't know the circumstances.

CONNIE: Like what?

BETTY: Like what if he was his best friend in the whole world? And made all types of sacrifices for him? And took care of him, like a brother, when he was young, or sick, and alone, and afraid.

CONNIE: Or maybe they are holding a gun to his head, and he knows that facing a little time in jail isn't anything compared to what they will do to him if he becomes a rat.

BETTY *(shivering)*: I hate that term.

CONNIE: Rat?

BETTY: The term. The animal. The thought. The concept. The teeth. The tail. *(with an emphasis on 'tail')* Everything about them.

CONNIE: At any rate….

BETTY: I actually really don't think that the Government should be able to do that.

CONNIE: Do what?

BETTY: Threaten to punish people who really don't deserve to be punished just so they can try to get someone who does deserve it.

CONNIE: Well, but they are probably saying that everyone who breaks the law deserves it; but we are going to go easy on some, not cuz we really want to, but just cuz we need to and it's better in the grand scheme of things, to let the little guy off, so they can get the really bad ones.

BETTY: Yeah, but they never seem to get the really bad ones.

CONNIE: No. *(taking a sip, shrugging)*

BETTY: I've still got to work up the nerve to confront that bastard who screwed Sally.

CONNIE: I thought you confronted him?

BETTY *shakes her head 'No'.*

CONNIE: Woman-Up!

BETTY *(after a brief pause)*: Sometimes I watch these people. Trying to get noticed. With gestures. They think they are making a difference.

CONNIE: Maybe they are.

BETTY: No they're not.

CONNIE: I don't know. I wouldn't underestimate the willingness of someone to simply take a stand. It's not a little thing.

BETTY *takes a sip.*

CONNIE: But Sally's okay, huh?

BETTY: Yeah, she's fine. We're the only ones that are pissed about it.

CONNIE: It's too bad Sally and Jenny didn't stay closer.

BETTY: You never know. I think a lot of kids who are childhood friends get into different cliques in high school; then the go off to college; but then they find themselves friends again after they graduate and start to come home.

CONNIE: I hope she'll have a place to call home.

BETTY *reaches for Connie's hand and presses it warmly.*

CONNIE *frowns.*

BETTY: I had this dream. Where Sally was a little girl. And she couldn't talk. But I could read her mind. And she needs money for something. So I go to give her some bills. And she shakes her head 'No'. And she's like this mendicant pan-handler. And I say: 'That's what you want? Money that makes noise? Okay, you can have all my money that makes noise.'

They laugh together.

CONNIE: When I have a dream about Jenny like that as a little girl, it's like I know that something is off. You want to enjoy the moment. But you can't, fully. And then you wake up. And you're thinking, 'What was off?' And then you realize: She's not three anymore.

BETTY: That's how it is: One minute they are running into your arms, with their soft little onesies, and the next minute they're all grown up.

CONNIE: It's just a cliché, until it happens to you. Then it's true.

BETTY: I think we all like to think that we're more unique than we really are.

CONNIE: 'Our acts are merely seven ages.'

BETTY *seems to acknowledge, gutturally. And then:* Well, Richard's addition is turning into a bad cliché.

CONNIE: Really? What's the problem?

BETTY: You gotta get approval. Someone doesn't like it. Someone else says it's too this or too that. Not enough parking. Not enough green space. Too much overhang. Then it goes to Court.

CONNIE: Really?

BETTY: Yeah, it's crazy. You start out wanting to do something, but then he spends all his time and money fighting about permits.

CONNIE: At least you got the fumigators to admit that they messed up and agree to re-treat everything.

BETTY *(raising her glass)*: Thank God for science.

CONNIE *laughs. And then:* Speaking of science, have you seen that Mother Earth television series.

BETTY: No, I've been meaning to.

CONNIE: You should tape it.

BETTY: I will, I will. Just need to remember.

CONNIE: Anyway, I was watching this segment on albinos, and they were talking about how they get shunned from their herds. And it's heartbreaking.

Because when you are watching, you can see that there isn't any real difference between them. But they can't see it.

BETTY: Scares me more and more as I get older.

CONNIE: That you'll turn into an albino? And be shunned by the Newberry society?

BETTY: No. *(and then)* It's silly. Forget it.

CONNIE: What?

BETTY: Dying alone.

CONNIE: Worse than that: What about living alone.

and she raises her eyebrows, as Betty sighs

OFFSTAGE, a telephone rings.

Connie gets up and leaves the stage.

The phone rings again.

CONNIE *(off-stage)*: Hello? …. Oh my God. That's terrible. …. We'll be right there. *(and she comes back into the kitchen, yelling)* Dad! …. Dad! …. Come on, we need to go!

BETTY: What is it?

CONNIE: His friend, Terry. They are rushing him to the hospital.

BETTY: Oh my God. I'm sorry.

CONNIE: Dad! … Dad! … Come on, we need to go!

Scene Three.

At the center of the stage is a fireplace with a brick mantle. Dusty wood floor. Charles and Jenny walk the room. Empty. No electricity.

CHARLES: Eerie, huh?

JENNY: The whole thing.

CHARLES: I mean I only met the guy once.

JENNY: I guess he just didn't have anyone else.

CHARLES: What about your family?

JENNY: It's just sad. Isn't it?

CHARLES: He seemed decently happy. Had your grandfather.

JENNY: And now I have to feel guilty, -

CHARLES: Why do you think he didn't leave it to him?

JENNY: - cuz I didn't even like the guy.

CHARLES: There's nothing for-

JENNY: Was mean to him.

CHARLES: Nah, you were fine.

JENNY is at the edge of the stage, looking off. And then says:

> What do you think the problem was? My mom said he couldn't have company. Doesn't seem that bad.

CHARLES: Maybe it was the stuff inside. *(and after a brief pause)* Or missing.

JENNY: What do you think about that stairway?

CHARLES *(following Jenny's gaze, off-stage)*: It does seem off.

JENNY: I think it's kinda cool. Different.

CHARLES: Why do you think it stands out?

JENNY *shrugs.* People like things that are symmetrical.

CHARLES: Or people hate things that are asymmetrical.

JENNY *raises here eyebrows.* Hmn.

CHARLES: You know what this place reminds me of?

JENNY: What?

CHARLES: When I was a kid, every year, we would go to this cabin with my family. And roast marshmallows. And watch the sunset.

JENNY: Sounds nice.

CHARLES: It's just a shitty little lake with shitty little fish. But when it's your lake, and your fish....

JENNY: Seems like everyone's got that place.

CHARLES: The reservoir.

JENNY: For some people.

CHARLES: Do you have a place like that?

JENNY: There was this rocky little beach in Maine we went to a couple times. Just a shitty little beach with shitty little rocks. And clammy fishy clams.

CHARLES: I can see your dad bitching about the cold water.

JENNY: No, he was good. He would carry me on his shoulders, and I would point down, and he would dig his hands in and scoop them.

CHARLES: And your mom would steam them?

JENNY: I'm not sure if she would do it, or if she would get the co-op to. But she would take me fishing in the mornings and we would catch these shitty little fish – which seemed like sparkly little rainbows that were heavier and scarier than they should have been, jumping around and trying to catch their breath.

CHARLES: And you would wander into the woods alone, and study the micrology.

JENNY: Yep. Spiders and blueberries.

CHARLES: Sounds like an alt-indie rock band.

JENNY: So what are you going to do with this place?

CHARLES: Good question.

JENNY: Is there a mortgage?

CHARLES: Nope. It's all paid up.

JENNY: I wonder what Terry ever even did? For a living.

CHARLES: Think he was like a store manager of some sort.

JENNY: It's hard to imagine him working.

CHARLES: He probably would have said the same about us.

JENNY: Do you think the Boomer Generation doesn't care about income inequality because they feel guilty about creating it and are therefore just in denial and don't want to think about the whole thing?

CHARLES: Maybe. *(and then)* I suspect that when you get to be an adult – a real adult – with family pressures and a job and all of that, you probably get kind of myopic about your own situation, and the only time you really even think about stuff like that is if you see some talking punt-head on CNBC; but even then it all seems abstract and irrelevant.

JENNY: But don't you care that Chad Tuckitt has like a townhouse in Brooklyn and a Mercedes convertible and eats at Nobu while single working mothers pulling two 30-hour shifts can barely scrape enough together to get their kids proper day care and make sure they have what they need for school?

CHARLES: I think some combination of labor and fortune will put different people into different places no matter what we try to do; and whether it's a hundred-to-one or a million-to-one, or only one-and-a-half-to-one, it will always sting, and never seem fair, and for the next thousands of years people rich or poor will always find something to feed their angst.

JENNY: So we should just live with systemic and institutional systems that – oh, yeah, as fate would have it – just happen to advantage you?

CHARLES: Not sure why we are fighting about this. Very kind of dorm-roomy thingy.

JENNY: And you are too old and mature for discussions like this now?

CHARLES: It's just tired.

JENNY: Sorry.

CHARLES: Doesn't change anything.

JENNY *says*: Most talking doesn't; but people still do it, *as* CHARLES *says:* and, for whatever it might be worth, I am not exactly sure that widespread is the same as institutional.

JENNY: I don't even –

CHARLES: Or systemic. You know?

JENNY: No, I don't know.

CHARLES: Just because it's widespread, or systemic, does that mean it's part of the design?

JENNY: So it's just natural selection, then? The way things are supposed to be?

CHARLES: It doesn't matter.

JENNY: Why not? It maters to me.

CHARLES: I just hate conversations like this.

JENNY *(sarcastically)*: Ohhhh, Sorry. So what does matter?

CHARLES: What about happiness?

JENNY: What about it?

CHARLES: Well, I have been thinking about people. People who are happy.

JENNY *(rolling her eyes)*: This will be good.

CHARLES: It just seems like people who seem miserable are people who are searching for the truth. And the people who seem happy are people who are only trying to win the game.

JENNY: So now you're not looking for the truth anymore? You're just going to play around? And hope you 'win' the 'game'?

CHARLES: No, *(thoughtfully),* I don't think you can change what kind of person you are.

JENNY: So you're just stuck being some tortured arrogant condescending truth-seeker who will never be happy or satisfied?

CHARLES: Probably.

JENNY: And am I ill-fated to the same doom?

CHARLES: Probably.

Jenny takes out her cellphone and starts to look through texts, or e-mails, or Facebook, or news feeds, or tweets.

Charles obliges, doing the same.

JENNY *(looking up and over at Charles)*: So you're just going to ignore me, and play on your cell?

CHARLES: You were just doing the exact same thing!

JENNY: Was not.

CHARLES *demonstrably shakes his head.*

JENNY: I read what you wrote by-the-way.

CHARLES: And?

JENNY: Not sure I know what you were trying to say.

CHARLES: Good.

JENNY: Why is it good that I didn't know what you were saying?

CHARLES: If you're not saying two things, you're not saying anything.

JENNY: Deep.

CHARLES: If you're not saying two things, (at least), you're not saying anything.

JENNY: Well, I didn't know either of the two or more things you were trying to say.

CHARLES: That's disappointing.

JENNY *(after taking a deep breath)*: So what are you going to do with this place?

CHARLES: Whatever you tell me.

Scene Four.

Living Room. There are cardboard boxes stacked around the room. Jacob is sitting in the la-z-boy recliner, Bill and Betty on the couch. Connie pacing around.

CONNIE: Where could she be?

BETTY: I'm sure she's fine.

BILL: Come on, sit down. You're making me dizzy.

CONNIE *(stopping the pacing for a minute and looking at Bill)*: This is your fault.

BILL: My fault?

CONNIE: Yes.

BILL: Getting fired? Or running off that Chaz kid?

CONNIE: I don't know!

BILL *appeals silently to Jacob.*

JACOB: I'm sure she's fine.

From off-stage a telephone rings, and Connie runs off-stage.

Betty gets up and follows her.

JACOB: I'm sure she's fine.

BILL: Yeah, it's all an over-reaction.

JACOB: You get the moving vans lined up?

BILL: Yep. *(and then)* You know, I wanted to apologize.

JACOB: To me?

BILL *nods his head 'Yes'.*

JACOB: Whatever for?

BILL: I just… particularly after what happened with Terry…. You shouldn't have to be moving at this point in your life.

JACOB: I'm fine, Bill. You've given me a home.

BILL: Just wanted to do more.

JACOB: Don't be silly.

And, after a moment:

BILL: Can I ask? … Are you hurt… that Terry….

JACOB: What?

BILL: Never mind.

Connie and Betty come back into the room.

BILL: Who was it?

CONNIE: Oh, just someone from the moving company. Not her.

BETTY *(gripping Connie's hand)*: She'll turn up. It'll be okay.

BILL: You tried her roommate, huh?

CONNIE: Went to voicemail, three times.

JACOB: I remember one time when Connie was just a little girl and we couldn't find her anywhere. We got the whole neighborhood together. All these parents and kids walking the streets with flashlights, yelling 'Connie', 'Constance dear'. Finally she wandered back home. She had chased a cat into a neighbor's yard.

CONNIE: Jumpstick

JACOB: Forlorn looking cat.

CONNIE: No she wasn't.

JACOB: So we asked her where she had been? Hiding in the neighbor's bushes. Didn't you hear everyone calling for you? 'Yes' she said, 'that's why I was hiding.' Why didn't you come out? 'You always tell me not to go to strangers.'

CONNIE: I loved that cat – and *(with an emphasis on 'and' and looking right at Jacob)* he was great at taking care of the mice.

JACOB: Birds too, though.

CONNIE: No he didn't.

JACOB: Just a couple. Your mom made sure to clean up and keep it hidden.

CONNIE *(after a pause, sadly)*: What kind of birds?

JACOB: I don't know. Robin. Blue jay.

BILL: I think I'm going to read a book.

CONNIE: Now?!?

BILL: Not this second. Just generally.

CONNIE: When is the last time you read a book?

BILL: I don't know.

BETTY: I am not sure that Richard has read an actual book since college.

BILL: I'm not sure I have either.

CONNIE: You haven't.

BILL: What should I read?

BETTY: What type of stuff do you like?

BILL: Not sure.

BETTY: Sorry, can't help you then.

BILL: I know I don't want to read anything about racism, sexism, harassment, slavery, addiction, immigrants, transgenders, or people who were molested when they were a child.

CONNIE: Good luck with that.

JACOB: Moneyball?

BETTY: I love that movie.

JACOB: It was a movie?

BETTY: Brad Pitt

BILL: Ah, of course.

JACOB: Need to see that.

CONNIE *(to Bill)*: I can't believe you're just sitting here, talking about books.

BILL: What do you want me to do?

CONNIE: You don't even read!

BILL: Wherever Jenny is, whatever she is doing, is not going to change anything whether I am reading or not reading or talking about reading or watching movies with the hotness or notness of Brad Pitt.

BETTY: Hey, we're all upset. I'm sure that Jennifer is fine. There's nothing anyone can do but wait. I'm sure that everything will be okay.

JACOB: Miss Betty, could I trouble you for a glass of water, please?

BETTY: Sure, *(as she leaves the stage).*

BILL *(calling)*: Can you please also bring me some corn chips?

CONNIE: Now you're eating corn chips?!?

BILL *(calling)*: Nix the chips.

CONNIE: I gotta get outta here.

And she exits.

BETTY *(coming back onto the stage carrying a glass of water)*: Where did she go?

BILL *shrugs.*

BETTY: Do you think I should go after her?

BILL *shrugs again.*

Betty hands the water to Jacob, who doesn't take it; but, rather, starts to stand.

JACOB: I'll go.

And he exits.

And Betty sits down on the couch with the glass of water next to Bill.

BETTY: You want those corn chips now?

And they laugh a bit.

BILL: You know what I was thinking?

BETTY: What?

BILL: If you were going to start a restaurant –

BETTY: Is that what you are planning to do?

BILL: No, not really. But if I were: You don't want to be the one who develops the property into the restaurant.

BETTY: You don't?

BILL: What do I know. But I don't think so. They always seem to spend a fortune, and make it beautiful, and everyone says they want to try it, but not enough of them actually do. And there is just this tremendous amount of overhead; so they get desperate. And have to sell. And then the next owner picks up a basically brand new restaurant for a song.

BETTY: Maybe.

BILL: What's the breach in my logic?

BETTY: I have no idea about the restaurant business. But I suspect that there is a bank standing behind it somewhere in there.

BILL: Ahhh, the bank….

BETTY: With a mortgage. And they are taking it over and want to get their money out of it, *(with an emphasis on 'their').* So maybe the second owner gets it for less, but I don't think they get it for a song.

BILL: You're so smart.

BETTY: Thank you.

BILL: Nothing's as simple as it seems.

BETTY: Or it's simpler.

From off-stage a telephone rings. Bill stands, and takes the glass of water from Betty, and exits the stage.

BILL *(from Off-Stage)*: Hello? .... Oh, great. What a relief. Thanks for calling.

And Bill comes back into the room.

BILL: She's fine, (*and he takes a cellphone out of his pocket*).

BETTY: Oh, great. That's a relief.

BILL *(into the cellphone)*: Connie? She's fine. .... I just heard from her roommate. .... She was apparently in class or something. .... No, the roommate. Jenny is driving, and didn't have a charge on her phone. .... I don't know. .... I don't know. .... I ... I ... I don't know. Just be relieved. .... Okay. *(and then to Betty)* Jesus.

BETTY: Such a relief.

BILL: Yeah.

BETTY *(smiling)*: You were never worried.

BILL: Not really. But then your mind starts wandering, and wondering. And worm-holing. And everyone's else's mind starts wandering and wondering and worm-holing. And it's kind of like this spiral-snowball effect.

BETTY: Well, it's over now. *(and after a brief pause)* How are you otherwise? We're going to miss you.

BILL: Sure we'll be back.

BETTY: Are you worried?

BILL: You know, I was thinking about it.

BETTY: Yeah?

BILL: And, really, for the first time in my life, there is nothing I really want.

BETTY: That must be liberating.

BILL: At first. But then it starts to feel more like despair.

BETTY: You don't seem depressed.

BILL: Who knows what that even means.

BETTY: I think it can be physical.

BILL: Maybe.

BETTY: You get sleepy all the time. Emotional. Not just sad, but… teary, almost. Well sad too. But then you also feel physical-type pain.

BILL: Have you ever been depressed?

BETTY: Well, sure, depressed in the colloquial sense. Don't think I've been clinically depressed.

BILL: But I seem that way to you?

BETTY: How would I know?

After a brief pause:

BILL: What I've noticed the most I think is the way I experience time.

BETTY: Time?

BILL: Yeah. I used to feel that I was moving through time. Now I kinda feel that I am just here, for my appointed hours. You know? I have to be here. While time is moving through me.

And after a brief pause:

Or around me.

And after another brief time:

BETTY: But, – I have to ask – but, you haven't ever thought of doing... anything stupid?

BILL: Not yet. *(and then)* I'm just joking.

BETTY: That isn't something to joke about.

BILL: People only joke about things that aren't anything to joke about.

BETTY: Huh, *(amused)*. Sally's old boyfriend had a knack for laughing inappropriately.

BILL: How is Sally?

BETTY: She's good. Active dating life.

BILL: Does that bother you?

BETTY: No, it's good.

BILL: Does it bother Richard?

BETTY: I think maybe a bit. But I think it's good. You need to not get too serious too young. Learn what you really want, what you really like. What's real and what's not real. *(and after a brief time)* What about you? Does Jenny dating – not Charles or anyone in particular, but just generally – being with men, bother you?

BILL: I used to think I would be all messed up about the virginity thing. But then once you have kids….

BETTY: What?

BILL: Then you realize…. It's like…

BETTY *waiting.*

BILL: There's nothing that she could do, that I wouldn't still love her.

BETTY: You should tell your daughter that.

BILL: I can't.

BETTY: Why not?

BILL: I don't know.

BETTY: Daughters and daddies.

BILL: And how is Richard, otherwise?

BETTY: I don't know.

BILL: What's wrong?

BETTY: Maybe nothing. But I see signs.

BILL: Signs of what?

BETTY: Or at least think I see signs.

BILL: I'm sure it's nothing.

BETTY: They say that people are quick to trade a disagreeable truth for a satisfying lie.

BILL: Of course what is truth.

BETTY: And is anyone ever really satisfied by the lie.

Connie and Jacob return to the stage. Jacob leans back into the la-z-boy, while Connie stands near Betty.

CONNIE: Have we heard anything further?

BILL: No, not yet.

CONNIE: Sorry about before.

BILL and BETTY: No problem.

CONNIE: I can't tell you how relieved I am.

BILL: Yep.

CONNIE: I don't understand, if her phone is out, how she got in touch with her roommate and not us?

BILL: I think she borrowed a phone from someone.

CONNIE: But why the roommate?

BETTY: Maybe she didn't realize you were so worried about her?

CONNIE: Yeah, that makes sense, I guess. …. Just want to hear her voice.

BETTY: So where did you guys go?

CONNIE: Just for a little walk.

JACOB: The maple leaves are really spiriting.

CONNIE: I didn't even notice.

BETTY: Tunnel vision, huh?

CONNIE: I just kept thinking, 'What if something happened to her?'

BETTY: Well, thank god she's okay.

CONNIE: Just paralyzing.

BILL: Can I eat my corn chips now?

CONNIE: J-E-N-N-Y!

And Jenny steps onto the stage, while Connie runs over to her and squeezes her fiercely.

As Charles trails in behind.

BILL: Hello, Charles. What are you doing here?

JENNY: Mom, Dad, I have some news. That's why we have been out of pocket.

And she holds up her finger to reveal a thin gold band with a micro diamond.

CHARLES: We eloped!

Scene Five.

Connie is alone in a cramped apartment with Jacob. Stage right is the la-z-boy recliner, where Jacob is sitting. Stage left and center is a kitchen behind a breakfast table and four wooden chairs, so that the kitchen, the breakfast/dining area, and the living room all blend together in one confined space. The kitchen space is L-shaped, so that Connie can stand at the far stage left counter fiddling around with dough with her side to the audience.

JACOB: It's the telling them not to.

CONNIE: What?

JACOB: You tell someone they can't do something they don't really care about too much, and all of the sudden they care about doing it a lot.

CONNIE: Is that directed at me?

JACOB: No. Of course not. Just making an observation.

CONNIE: Are you going to eat some of these cookies?

JACOB: Of course. If you let me.

CONNIE: What are you talking about? Why wouldn't I let you? I am making them for you. And Bill.

JACOB: If you say so.

CONNIE: Okay, whatever, get back to your tv.

JACOB: Hey.

Connie turns to look at him.

CONNIE *(impatiently)*: Yeah?

JACOB: When you were five, you asked me if you were adopted.

CONNIE: And?

JACOB: I said, 'Not yet.'

CONNIE *(turning back to the counter)*: Funny.

JACOB: So let me ask you: Who knew what time it was when the first clock was made?

CONNIE *snorts.* Hah, hah, hah.

JACOB: Why is there a D in 'fridge' but not in 'refrigerator'?

CONNIE *shakes her head.* I don't know, dad.

JACOB: Why is it that, a hundred years ago everyone owned a horse, and only rich people owned cars; but now everyone owns a car, and only rich people own horses?

CONNIE: Why is a spinning mouse?

JACOB: How is a hamster.

A brief silence.

CONNIE: Do you think mom liked your jokes?

JACOB: Why do you say 'do I think'? Sounds like you already know the answer.

CONNIE: Oh, I do know. I just want to know what you think.

JACOB: I think she probably found them both annoying and endearing.

CONNIE *nods.*

JACOB: Am I right?

CONNIE: In the beginning, she found them cute and differentiating. Over time, she found them increasingly irritating. Perhaps later, I think she would find them either charming or exasperating, (but not both), *(emphasis on 'both'),* depending on how well you were getting along at the time.

JACOB *turns back from looking over at Connie to the audience and the would-be tv. And says:*

This person is such a nimrod.

CONNIE: What is he saying?

JACOB: Something about how climate change is a hoax because carbon dioxide cannot mix well in the atmosphere.

CONNIE: Everyone has the right to his or her own opinion.

JACOB: Yeah, but that doesn't mean you put them on air to broadcast it.

CONNIE: You get what you pay for.

JACOB: Not usually.

CONNIE *continues to knead the dough.*

JACOB: These so-called 'experts' they drum up are no better than a donkey throwing darts at a windmill.

CONNIE: Well change the channel. Or read a book. Go outside. No one's twisting your arm.

JACOB: I like my game show.

CONNIE: Not on?

JACOB: Not til 6:00.

CONNIE: Can probably get on demand.

JACOB: I don't think we have that on this new system.

CONNIE: Oh, sorry.

A long pause.

JACOB: Just grateful to be here, Connie. I really am.

And after another brief pause:

CONNIE: Of course, we could be living in Terry's old house....

JACOB *does not reply.*

CONNIE: It just goes against ... every ... any thing.

JACOB *does not reply.*

CONNIE: But....

What are we going to do? Throw you into one of those old folks homes?

JACOB: Assisted living facilities.

CONNIE: You don't need assistance.

JACOB: Not yet.

CONNIE: That's cheery.

And, after a pause:

We couldn't afford it even if we wanted to anyway.

And then:

JACOB: When the time comes, I don't want you wasting your life cleaning up after me.

CONNIE: Don't be silly.

JACOB: I'm serious.

CONNIE: Well, let's cross that banister when the stairs get a little steeper.

JACOB: Connie.

CONNIE *(turning)*: What?

JACOB: I'm serious.

CONNIE: Um-hum.

JACOB: I don't want to be a burden.

CONNIE: It's not a burden, dad. It's life.

JACOB: We spend all this time and money to keep people alive long enough so that they get to the stage where they'd just assume move on.

CONNIE: Come on, pop. We're not doing so bad.

JACOB: No, sweetie. Just missing your mom. That's all.

CONNIE *wipes a tear from her cheek.*

JACOB: And I know you miss her more than I do.

CONNIE: We both miss her.

A brief silence.

JACOB: What's the word from Jenny?

BILL *comes onto the stage from stage right, and says* Hello Jacob *as he passes the recliner and makes his way over to one of the wooden chairs at the dining table. He is dressed in a suit and has loosened his tie.*

CONNIE *(without turning)*: Hey.

BILL *(loosening his tie further)*: People say that the sign of genius is the ability to hold two opposing ideas at the same time. But it's really quite common.

JACOB: No luck?

CONNIE: You're in a mood.

BILL: Who knows. They're always friendly to your face. Always make you think you're going to get it. But then they never call.

CONNIE *exhales deeply, placing the tray of cookies into the oven, getting a can of diet soda from the refrigerator, and sitting in one of the other wooden chairs; her side to Bill.*

BILL: Any word from the honeymooners?

CONNIE: Nope.

BILL: Not long before they make you mow the lawn. And she has to start wearing pajamas.

CONNIE: When have you ever mowed a lawn in your life?

BILL: Metaphorically.

JACOB: Can find something worse than mowing the lawn, can't you?

BILL: Let me think on it.

JACOB: What about taking out the trash?

BILL: Nah, that doesn't take too long.

JACOB: Walking the dog?

BILL: Never had one.

JACOB: Metaphorically.

BILL *goes to the refrigerator and gets a bottle of beer. Asking:*

You want anything, Jacob?

JACOB: Think I'll lean on the lorry for now.

And Bill sits back down with his beer at the table.

BILL *(to Connie)*: Did you hear what happened to Everett?

CONNIE: No, what?

BILL: Stroke.

CONNIE: Oh, no.

BILL: Was with the kids.

CONNIE: That's terrible.

BILL: They saw the whole thing.

CONNIE: I can't imagine.

Silence.

JACOB: Every life is a tragedy.

More silence.

BILL *(to Connie)*: You know what I don't understand?

CONNIE: What?

BILL: Jenny has a lot of girl friends.

CONNIE: And?

BILL: So why did she need to feel the need to do it?

CONNIE: Girlfriends are nice. But at some point during the wedding, you want to get up and marry the groom.

BILL *(shaking his head and making an 'I give up' or 'what?' with his hands)*: I have no idea what your saying.

JACOB: It's metaphorical.

CONNIE *(turning to Bill)*: What's done is done. I don't agree with it any more than you do. And who knows what will happen in the future. But don't make me choose between you and our daughter. Cuz I think you know who is going to lose.

BILL: I won't.

CONNIE: You are.

BILL: How? What am I doing? What am I making you choose?

CONNIE: You're not …

BILL: What?! First I am; now I'm not. What?

CONNIE: You're not liste-

BILL: Yes I am! You said I am 'making you choose'! But I'm not. We're just here. And she's there. With Chaz. In Terry's house. While we are in this shitty little apartment, -

CONNIE: Stop.

BILL: And who knows how long we can even afford that?!

CONNIE *starts to speak*

BILL: And I didn't choose any of it, *(with an emphasis on 'choose')*. And neither did you. So how I am making you -

CONNIE: STOP!

> *And then, she says, teary, and tapping her chest:*

> In my heart.

> *Silence.*

BILL: Okay.

> *And he stands, and steps over to Connie, and kisses her softly on the cheek.*

> Okay.

JACOB: Well now that that's all settled, when are those delicious-smelling cookies going to be ready?

CONNIE *chuckles to herself a bit, wiping her eye. And then says:* Thirty-seven minutes.

BILL *(to Jacob)*: Your game show on?

JACOB: No, not yet.

BILL: May be preempted by the baseball game.

JACOB: Oh, don't tell me.

CONNIE *looks at Bill, and takes a deep breath*: What are we going to do?

BILL: It will work out.

CONNIE: How?

BILL: Jacob's going to go onto that game show and win us a fortune.

CONNIE: That's your plan?

BILL: Maybe Chaz will die and leave us the house?

CONNIE *(shaking her head, and turning back towards Jacob)*: Didn't you apply once, daddy?

JACOB: Not really.

BILL: I bet you would make it.

CONNIE: Could win some money.

JACOB: I wouldn't make it; but... It would... adulterate the sanctity of it.

BILL: 'Adulterate'? The 'sanctity' of it? *(emphasis on 'sanctity')*

JACOB: In a way.

BILL: It's a television show, for god's sakes.

JACOB: It's hard for me to explain.

BILL *rolls his eyes.*

CONNIE: They actually say it's good to exercise your brain like that.

JACOB: 'Life is not a drill.'

BILL: It's a game.

CONNIE: No, haven't you heard? It's all just a big computer simulation.

JACOB: ...but a dream.

FROM OFFSTAGE *(tv football coach)*: "...after all the goddamn shenanigans you pulled last season, you should be thanking God that you're still in a goddamn uniform, god damnit!"

CONNIE: What is this?

BILL: It's a parody of bad teen movies.

JACOB: At what point are they no longer making fun of bad teen movies, and actually just making a bad teen movie?

BILL *takes a sip of beer, and checks his watch. And then, to Jacob*: I think it should be on now if it's not preempted.

Jacob works the remote control.

FROM OFFSTAGE: You shake a Manhattan to fox trot time, but you use waltz time to shake a dry one of these.

JACOB: Martini

FROM OFFSTAGE: A flock of geese when not flying.

JACOB: Gaggle

CONNIE: What are they called when they are flying?

BILL: Dead meat.

FROM OFFSTAGE: William Shatner has a secret daughter in ads for this discount travel site.

JACOB: Priceline.com

FROM   OFFSTAGE: "Illumination   from   one underground passage's terminus"

JACOB: Light at the end of the tunnel.

FROM OFFSTAGE: "Maintain one's digits folded"

JACOB: Keep your fingers crossed....

And so it goes...

AUTHOR'S NOTES

ACT ONE

Scene One

Jenny is combining/conflating characters from two different television sitcoms from the 1970s. "Archie Bunker" is the central character from *All in the Family* (1971-1979), while "Grady" is the best friend and frequent houseguest/companion of Fred G. Sanford, of *Sanford & Son* (1972-1977). Archie Bunker was a working class husband and father living in Astoria, New York, frequently described by fans (although not without some rebuke) as a "lovable bigot". The show was considered groundbreaking, addressing openly issues such as racism, religion, women's lib, infidelity, homosexuality, abortion, miscarriage, rape, and the war in Vietnam. Sandford and his son, Lamont, owned and operated a junkyard in the driveway adjacent to their home in the Watts section of LA. Lovably bigoted and cantankerous, Fred was the black NBC answer to CBS' Bunker. Interestingly, though airing on competing networks, both sitcoms were developed by Norman Lear, who got the idea for both shows from across the pond, with *All in the Family* modelled on the British sitcom *Till Death Us Do Part,* which aired on BBC1 from 1965 to 1975, and *Sanford & Son* inspired by the BBC Television program *Steptoe & Son,* which ran in the U.K. from 1962 to 1965.

Scene Two

"Thunder Road" is the opening track on Bruce Springsteen's third studio album, *Born to Run* (Columbia 1975). In 1986, they released a five-album box set of live recordings called *Live/1975-85.* The collection opens with

"Ladies and gentlemen, Bruce Springsteen and the E Street Band," followed by a pared down version of Thunder Road recorded on October 18, 1975, at the Roxy Theatre, in West Hollywood, California.

In 2017, Springsteen opened on Broadway with an intimate and highly acclaimed one-man show, in which he played acoustic versions (some on piano, most on guitar) of fifteen of his songs, in a somewhat chronological narrative, interspersed and introduced with fragments and tales from his own life, as a coda to the publication of his autobiography *Born to Run* in 2016. The show was originally supposed to run from October to November of 2017, but the demand was so high, (face value tickets of $700 typically going in the secondary market for $3,000 or higher), additional dates were added through June of 2018, and extended again through December. A film version of the concert was made available thru Netflix and a *Springsteen on Broadway* album/CD was released.

"Living Proof" is the seventh track on Bruce Springsteen's tenth studio album, *Lucky Town* (Columbia 1992). While an acoustic guitar version of Thunder Road was included in the On Broadway play/concert/album/Netflix special, (in the *Live/1975-85* version Springsteen had been accompanied by Roy Bittan on the piano, along with someone in the background playing something that sounds like a xylophone), Living Proof – a more obscure tune, not typically performed in concert – was not. (it's God's love; in a world that's dark and fouled, dirty and confused; sometimes, if you look for it, living evidence and proof)

Re: Charles' think tank project, *see, e.g.,* Ecologic, "Post-Carbon Cities of Tomorrow in the US (POCACITO in the US)" https://www.ecologic.eu/12706 (June 10, 2020).

The Unabomber killed three people and injured twenty-three more in a series of sixteen domestic terrorist attacks beginning in the late Seventies. In 1995, he sent a "manifesto" titled *Industrial Society and its Future* to major newspapers outlining the ways in which technology was destroying the world and arguing that people should abandon the complexities of modern society and return to agrarian tribes. A linguistics professor, Roger Shuy, determined from some of the references in this Manifesto that the suspect (identified by the FBI with the case name UNABOM, for University and Airline Bomber) had roots in the Chicago area. The bomber's brother and sister-in-law (who had already harbored some suspicions) also recognized similarities between the Manifesto and some of his previous writings. All leading, with other bits of evidence, to his capture in 1996. It turned out that he was, in fact, Ted Kaczynski, a mathematical prodigy who grew up in Chicago before going to Harvard and becoming a professor. In the late 1960s, he abandoned his academic career and moved to a remote cabin in Montana without electricity or running water. For three years, while at Harvard, Kaczynski had participated in a brutal psychological experiment led by Henry Murray. Subjects were encouraged to write essays detailing their aspirations and beliefs, under the impression that they would be engaged with other students in personal discussions and debates. The essays, however, were turned over to an anonymous attorney who would use their contents to confront and belittle the students while electrodes monitored their physiological reactions. Kaczynski spent approximately 200 hours over the course of the study being systematically humiliated and verbally abused. Some sources have suggested that these experiments were part of Project MKUltra, the Central Intelligence Agency's research into mind control. Some have also suggested that this experience may have contributed to Kaczynski's criminal activities.

"Big" Sean Michael Leonard Anderson is the Detroit native whose rap album *I Decided* debuted at Number One on the Billboard charts in 2017. Jay-Z, as everyone knows, is from Brooklyn. (*Empire State of Mind*) [apparently,

Jay-Z's real name is also Shawn, but spelled with a "w":
Shawn Corey Carter] [and of course "P. Diddy"/"Puff
Daddy"'s name is also Sean: Sean John "Puffy" Combs]
[maybe there is just something about the name]

Wuthering Heights is an 1847 novel by Emily Bronte. It's
one of those old Gothic Victorian type things where an
orphan is taken in by a family and falls in love with the
daughter who also loves him but she won't marry him
because he's poor and so he goes off and becomes rich and
returns to take revenge on her but then realizes he messed
up and is haunted by her ghost, or something. Kate Bush
wrote a song called "Wuthering Heights" in 1978, which
was later covered by Pat Benatar on her album *Crimes of
Passion.*

Scene Three

Renoir's Boating Party is actually titled "Luncheon of the
Boating Party" (1881). There is also "A Boating Party" by
John Singer Sargent (1889) and "The Boating Party" by
Mary Cassatt (1893).

The English Romantic artist J.M. William Turner set a
number of paintings in Venice; his most well-known is
probably "from the Porch of Madonna Della Salute"
(1835).

Georgia O'Keeffe was a 20th Century artist best known for
her paintings of New York skyscrapers, New Mexico
landscapes, vagina-like flowers, and desert-bleached
bones.

Eminem (Marshall Mathers) is a white rapper who played
the role of "Bunny" (himself) in the 2002 biopic, *8 Mile.*
Supposedly accepted as 'authentic'/'real'/'down' by
blacks, he seems to have been very popular among
hip/cool wannabe white kids, either as an alternative or
initiation/gateway to more hard-core ('urban') ('ghetto')
('gansta') fare.

I was introduced to U2 *Live: Under a Blood Red Sky* during my freshman year of high school by either Satoshi Kitahama and/or Farrel Weil. The band reached the height of popularity in 1987 with *Joshua Tree,* but their best album was *The Unforgettable Fire* back in 1984. The group has continued to ride a global wave of success over the decades with poppy/alternative-rock sounding songs like *Beautiful Day* (2000) and albums/CDs like *How to Dismantle an Atomic Bomb* (2004).

Bend It Like Beckham is a romantic sports comedy from 2002 which follows an 18-year-old British girl obsessed with David Beckham and football (soccer). Her parents, of Indian Sikh descent, have forbidden her from playing because she is a girl; but she nevertheless joins a local women's team and makes her way to the top of the league. I don't remember the plot, but I am sure that everything probably works out and the parents eventually accept her. There is probably also some kind of a love story, which probably also ends favorably. (at least in the short term)

Million Dollar Baby is a movie that was directed by Clint Eastwood and stars Hillary Swank as a scrappy too-old boxer who breaks her neck and becomes bed-strapped and paralyzed. Can't remember what happens, but I am pretty sure it's a tear-jerker with a lot of regret and redemption and what probably feels to some like grace.

The oft-quoted and sometimes mis-quoted first sentence of Tolstoy's great novel *Anna Karenina* is: "Happy families are all alike; every unhappy family is unhappy in its own way" (Russia, 1877).

Scene Four

John Morgan wrote a book called *You Can't Teach Hungry,* sub-titled *Creating the Multimillion Dollar Law Firm,* in 2011.

Oliver Morgan (no relation) was born and raised in the Lower Ninth Ward of New Orleans, along with Fats Domino, Smiley Lewis, and Jessie Hill. In 1961, he released a debut single under the pseudonym "Nookie Boy". His one hit nationally, *Who Shot the La La,* was released in 1964, referring to the mysterious death of singer Lawrence "Prince La La" Nelson, in 1963. [The person we all know as "Prince" (l/k/a "The Artist Formerly Known as 'Prince'") could have possibly been related somehow to La La, born Prince Rogers Nelson and, at least according to wikipedia (citing Megan Smolenyak in the *Huffington Post* (Feb. 8, 2013)), all four of his grandparents hailed from Louisiana.]

Robert Parker started his career as a saxophonist who played with Professor Longhair on *Mardi Gras In New Orleans* in 1949. He had his biggest hit with *Barefootin'* which made the pop charts in Britain and sold over a million copies in 1965.

Al Johnson had a hit with *Carnival Time* in 1960.

Jessie Hill started out as a drummer for Professor Longhair and Huey "Piano" Smith. In 1960, his song *Ooh Poo Pah Doo* sold 800,000 copies and reached No. 3 on the Billboard R&B charts. His follow-up *Whip It On Me* apparently also made the Billboard Hot 100, topping out at ninety-three. [When we were in high school and college, we used to go see J.D. Hill (and the Jammers – and/or sometimes with Cyril Neville and his Uptown All Stars) at Benny's Bar, on Camp and Valance. Have no idea whether J.D. Hill was related to Jessie "Ooh Poo Pah Doo" Hill (?)]

The Big Bopper (J.P. Richardson, Jr.) was both a musician and a disc jockey. He was best known for *Chantilly Lace* (1958). He died in the same plane crash with Buddy Holly and Ritchie Valens around Clear Lake, Iowa, in 1959.

Fats Domino was much bigger and much earlier then Chubby Checker. Breaking out in 1949 with *The Fat Man,* Domino had five early gold records and then another thirty-five which reached the U.S. Billboard Top 40. Chubby Checker came along in 1960 with *The Twist,* (apparently a cover of something that had been previously recorded by Hank Ballard & The Midnighters).

John Henry, according to folklore, was the biggest/baddest/best steel-driver of his time. Someone set up a contest between him and a steam-powered machine to see who could dig a railway tunnel through the core of a mountain (Big Bend Mountain) the fastest. John Henry won the contest, only to drop dead of exhaustion. In the beginning of *John Henry Days,* (and presumably as a nod to the Prologue of *Moby Dick*), Colson Whitehead provides a number of different accounts of the legend. Personally, I have always been partial to the version on *The Essential ODETTA* LP (Vanguard 1973).

Scene Five

'Women who seek to be equal with men lack ambition' – Timothy Leary

Gilgamesh is often described as the most ancient surviving work of epic literature. Begun as long ago as Two Millennia B.C., and finished around 700 B.C., the story was discovered on 12 clay tablets in 1849 in what is now Iraq. In the standard Akkadian *Epic of Gilgamesh,* the central character is a demigod of superhuman strength who befriends a wild man named Enkidu. Together, they go on adventures, defeating Humbaba and the Bull of Heaven, who is sent to attack them by Ishtar after Gilgamesh rejects her offer for him to become her consort. After Enkidu dies of a disease sent as punishment from the gods, Gilgamesh becomes afraid of his own death, and visits the sage Utnapishtim, the survivor of the Great Flood, hoping to find immortality. Gilgamesh repeatedly fails the trials set before him and returns home to Uruk, realizing that immortality is likely beyond his grasp.

ACT TWO

<u>Scene One</u>

Girl with a Pearl Earring is an iconic oil painting from the Dutch Golden Age by Johannes Vermeer (*circa* 1665). The subject's model was fictionalized in 1999 by Tracy Chevalier in a historical novel that was made into a film directed by Peter Webber in 2003.

The Eastman Kodak Company, founded in 1888, filed for Chapter 11 in 2012. Emerging from Bankruptcy in 2013, Kodak sold many of its patents to a group of companies that include Apple, Google, Facebook and Amazon. Personalized Imaging and Document Imaging are now part of Kodak Alaris, a separate company owned by the Kodak Pension Plan. In response to the Covid-19 Pandemic, the company announced that it would enter the pharmaceutical business.

Reading Gaol was a prison located in Berkshire, England. Oscar Wilde was incarcerated there after being convicted of gross indecency and sentenced to two years hard labor. Section VI of *The Ballad of Reading Gaol* (1897) begins: "In Reading Gaol by Reading Town there is a pit of shame, and in it lies a wretched man eaten by teeth of flame." The lines recall Charles Wooldridge, who slit his wife's throat and was hanged at the facility while Wilde was imprisoned there. The poem returns to the notion that "each man kills the thing he loves" – some by sword, others with a kiss.

"To the artist in love, a woman's face is only a suggestion of what her portrait could be" - Haley Mlotek, "Catalogue Raisonne" *NYT Book Review,* March 22, 2020 (reviewing *The Exhibition of Persephone Q* by Jessi Jezewska Stevens (2020)).

Emma's riddle comes from the Jane Austen novel (1815), wherein a suitor poses the following to the title character: "My first displays the wealth and pomp of kings, Lords of the earth! their luxury and ease. Another view of man, my second brings, Behold him there, the monarch of the seas!" Which she solves: "Courtship".

The founder of Martha Stewart Living Omnimedia, Stewart gained success in the 1980s and 90s through a number of bestselling books, the *Martha Stewart Living* magazine, and the syndicated *Martha Stewart Living* television program. In December 2001, Stewart avoided the loss of $45,673 when she sold all her shares of ImClone stock in advance of an adverse FDA ruling based on a call from her broker at Merrill Lynch. She was not convicted on the criminal insider trading charges, but was found guilty of obstruction and making false statements to federal investigators, for which she served five months in prison. An additional securities fraud charge, alleging that Stewart boosted the stock of her own company, was dismissed. While imprisoned, Stewart's jailhouse nickname is reputed to be 'M. Diddy'.

Scene Two

In *Jacobellis v. State of Ohio,* the U.S. Supreme Court was called upon to review the obscenity conviction of a theater manager who screened a French film, *Les Amants* ('*The Lovers*') (1958). Justice Brennan, writing for the majority, observes that the motion picture "involves a woman bored with her life and marriage who abandons her husband and family for a young archaeologist with whom she has suddenly fallen in love. There is an explicit love scene in the last reel of the film, and the State's objections are based almost entirely upon that scene. The film was favorably reviewed in a number of national publications, although disparaged in others, and was rated by at least two critics of national stature among the best films of the year in which it was produced. It was shown in approximately 100

of the larger cities in the United States, including
Columbus and Toledo, Ohio. We have viewed the film, in
the light of the record made in the trial court, and we
conclude that it is not obscene." 378 U.S. 184, 195-196
(1964). The decision is best known, however, for the
concurring opinion of Justice Potter Stewart, who, after
noting that the Court has been tasked with attempting to
define something that may indeed be indefinable (hard-
core pornography), famously said: "I know it when I see
it."

"All the world's a stage, And all the men and women
merely players; They have their exits and their entrances;
And one man in his time plays many parts, His acts being
seven ages." – William Shakespeare, *As You Like It* (Act
II, Scene Seven) (*circa* 1599)

"Thank God for science" - Amy Haible, Harpswell,
Maine. *NYT Magazine*, "The Thread" (*i.e.* Letters)
8/9/20, p.5.

Scene Three

'Chadtucket' is a trust fund bearing, pastel wearing,
Sunday scaries in his Sperry's, vodka soda drinking, dad's
yacht sinking, preppy, with tucked-in shorts, who graces
the island of Nantucket in the summer months with his
Sorority girlfriend or Frat Boy friends.

Scene Four

Moneyball: The Art of Winning an Unfair Game is a work
of non-fiction by Michael Lewis published in or around
2003 which was made into a movie directed by Bennett
Miller and starring Brad Pitt in 2011.

Scene Five

Joe Bastardi, a meteorologist appearing on Fox News,
argued that Carbon Dioxide "literally" cannot cause
warming because it doesn't "mix well in the atmosphere"

(it does). He's also claimed that warming would violate the First Law of Thermodynamics, which states that energy can neither be created nor destroyed. (In fact, global warming has nothing to do with newly created energy, but with the atmosphere trapping energy that's already around.) - Brooke Jarvis, "The 10 Dumbest Things Ever Said About Global Warming" *Rolling Stone* (June 19, 2013).

People who make their living "commenting or offering advice on political and economic trends" make poorer predictions than dart-throwing monkeys. *See* Daniel Kahneman, *Thinking, Fast and Slow* (2011); *see also, e.g.,* James Surowiecki, "Punditonomics" *New Yorker* (April 7, 2014); Douglas Starr, "The Interview" *New Yorker* (Dec. 9, 2013); Malcolm Gladwell, *Blink* (2013).

"...after all the goddamn shenanigans you pulled last season, you should be thanking God that you're still in a goddamn uniform, god damnit!" – The Coach, *Not Another Teen Movie,* directed by Joel Gallen (Columbia Pictures 2001).

"At what point are we no longer reenacting churning butter and actually just churning butter?" is the caption of a cartoon by Zachary Kanin in the *New Yorker* (Aug. 17, 2020).

Steve Herman
New Orleans, LA
November 2, 2020

Steve Herman was born and raised in New Orleans, Louisiana, where he attended Isidore Newman School. He received a Bachelor of Arts degree from Dartmouth College, where he was awarded Citations of Excellence in the study of Milton and Shakespeare, and won the Eleanor Frost Playwriting Competition with his one-act play *The Phoenix Sleeps Tonight.* Herman was then named Order of the Coif at Tulane Law School, where he graduated magna cum laude in 1994. After graduating from Tulane, Herman clerked for Justice Harry T. Lemmon of the Louisiana Supreme Court. He now practices law in New Orleans, where he was, among other things, Co-Lead Counsel for Plaintiffs in the BP Oil Spill Litigation.

Books by Steve Herman

AMERICA AND THE LAW:
CHALLENGES FOR THE 21ST CENTURY

THE GORDIAN KNOT

THE SIGN OF FOUR

A DAY IN THE LIFE OF TIMOTHY STONE

BROKEN LIGHTHOUSE

SHOTS ACROSS THE BOW

Coming Soon
PARABLES OF JOY

Visit:
www.gravierhouse.com

Made in the USA
Monee, IL
15 August 2022